# Tools

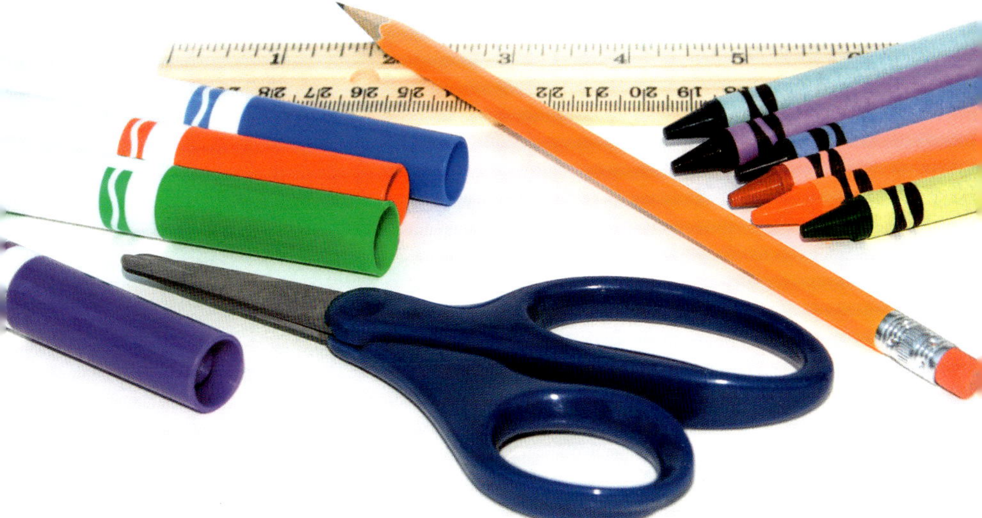

by Kris Bonnell

Here is a pencil.
A pencil is a tool.

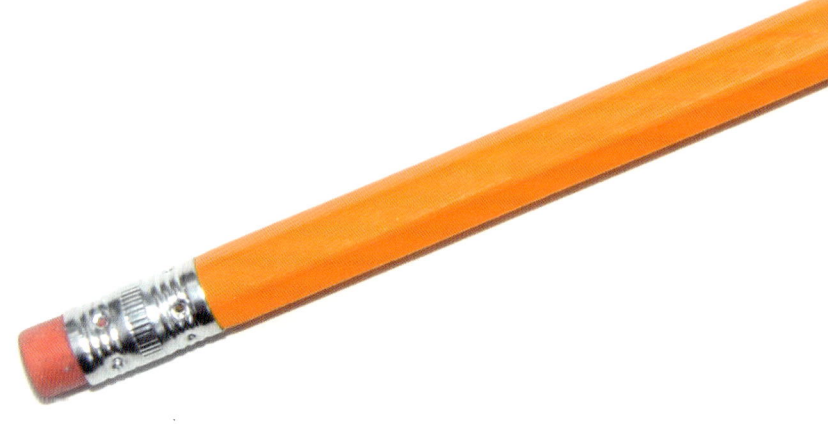

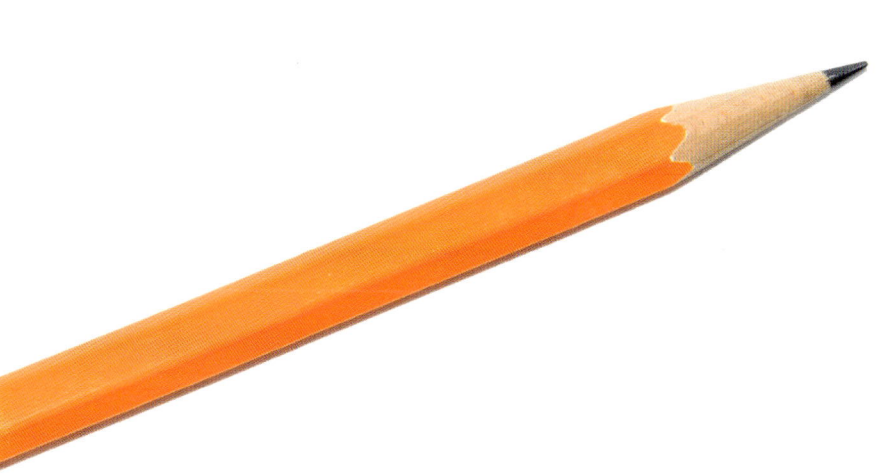

Here are crayons.

Crayons are tools.

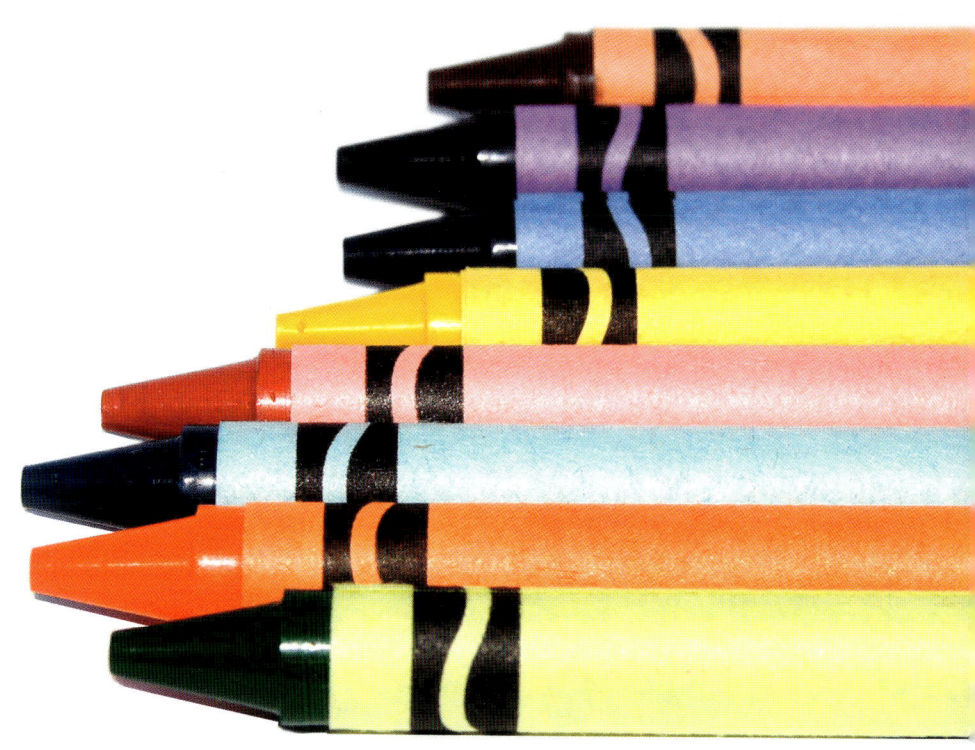

Scissors are tools.

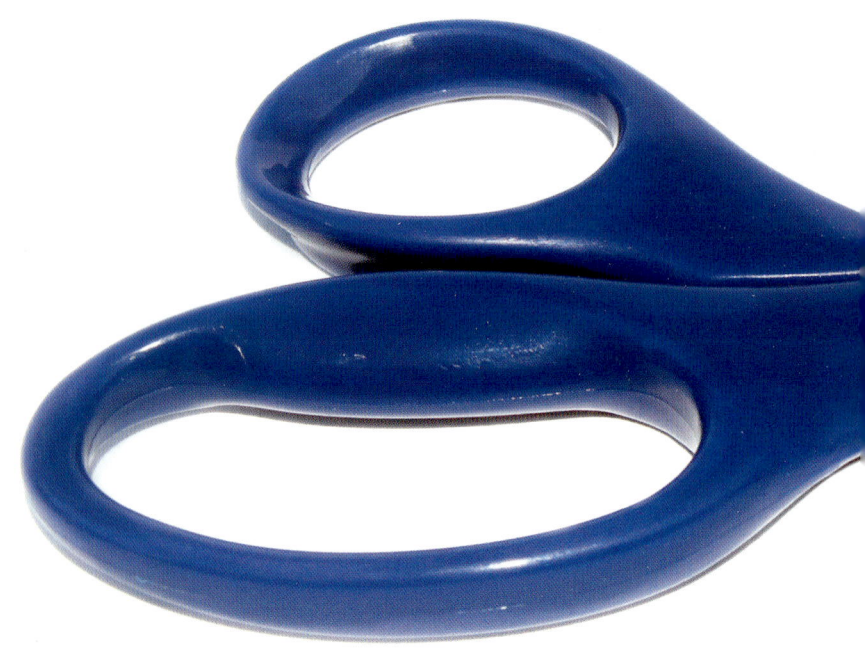

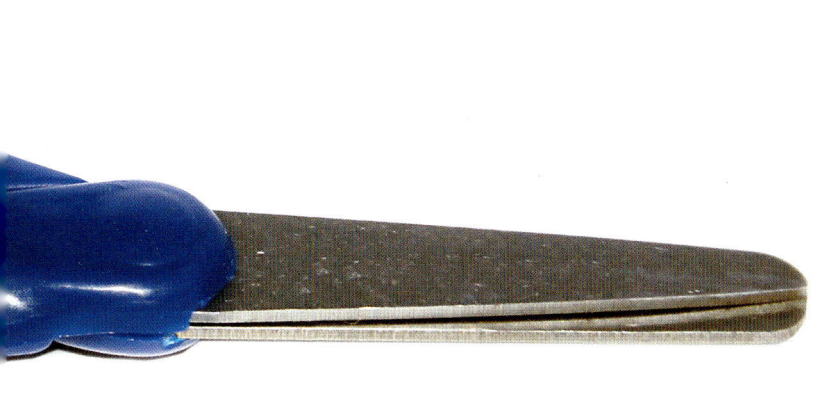

8

Here is a ruler.

A ruler is a tool.

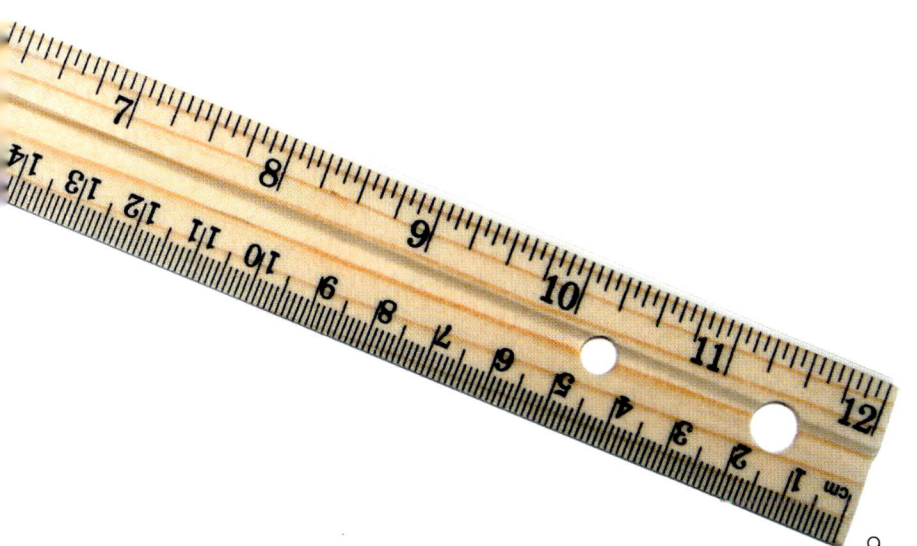

Markers are tools, too.

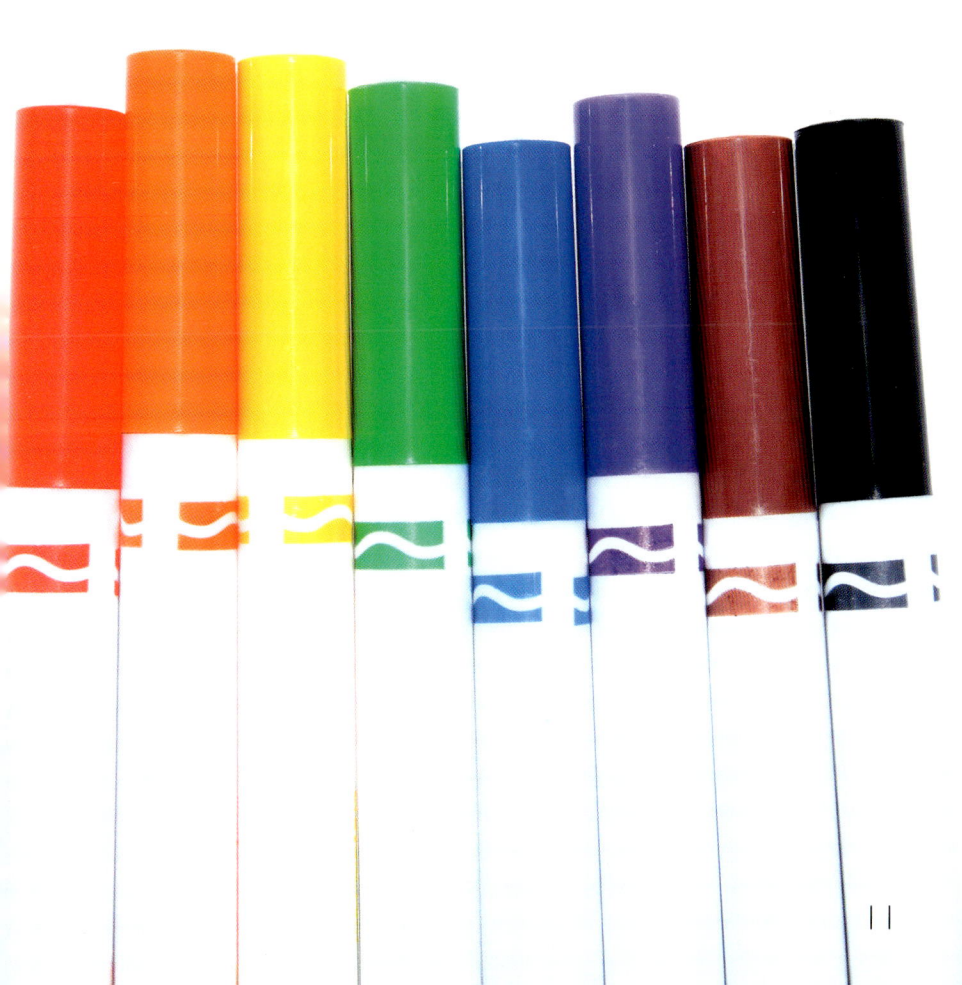

Here are tools for school!

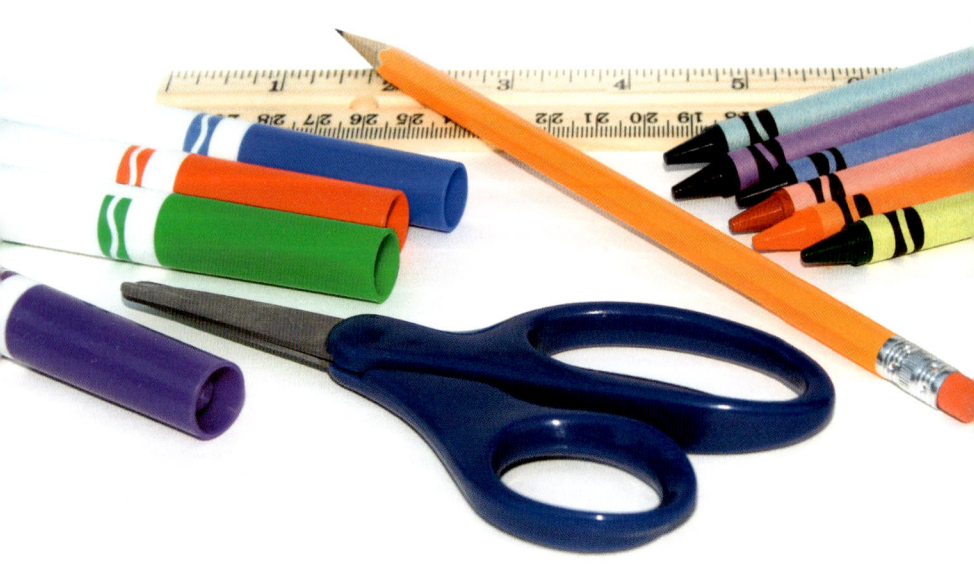